LAS VEGAS TRAVEL GUIDE FOR WOMEN

For Women, by Women: The Insider's Guide to the "Entertainment Capital of the World"

By Erica Stewart

ERICA STEWART

© **Copyright 2015**

All rights reserved. No part of this book may be reproduced or transmitted in any form or by any means, electronically or mechanically, including photocopy, recording, or by and information storage or retrieval system, without the written permission from the publisher, except in the case of brief quotations embodied in critical articles or reviews.

Trademarks are the property of their respective holders. When used, trademarks are for the benefit of the trademark owner only.

DISCLAIMER

The information provided herein is stated to be truthful and consistent, in that any liability, in terms of inattention or otherwise, by any usage or abusage of any policies, processes, or directions contained within is the solitary and utter responsibility of the recipient reader. Under no circumstances will any legal responsibility or blame be held against the publisher for any reparation, damages, or monetary loss due to the information herein, either directly or indirectly. Respective authors hold all rights not held by publisher.

Note from the Author:

Welcome to Sin City!

Contrary to what many believe, Las Vegas is not all strip shows, sinning and gambling, although there is still plenty of all three to go around. Nowadays, Las Vegas is so much more than that. It's the city that never sleeps, never stays the same and never stops gifting unforgettable experiences. The neon-overdose, food extravaganza, shopping emporiums and myriad of totally unique attractions have made this the #1 holiday destination in the whole U.S.A. - even if we do say so ourselves.

A woman's haven, Las Vegas boasts infinite fun whether you're travelling solo or with a group of girlfriends. Shop 'till you drop on The Strip, watch world-class shows, admire awe-inspiring resorts and collect memories that'll last a lifetime.

ERICA STEWART

Just hop onboard our Vegas express guide to this fabulous city and discover the pleasures this incredible Nevada treasure has to offer.

Chapter Index
Chapter 1: What to know before you go 10

    Yes. There is a seedy side to Vegas 10

    Every hotel lobby is amazing 11

    Small and compact...but huge 11

    Research where you want to stay 12

    ...but search for deals first 13

    Factor in the hidden 'Resort Fees' 14

    On a tight budget? Stay Downtown…...................... 14

    Use your usual 'common sense' safety precautions 15

    Wear comfy shoes & use free shuttles 15

    Enjoy the 24/7 life 16

    Look out for flyers and giant minions 16

    The traffic is manic 17

    Drink plenty of water 17

    Want to gamble? Take a class 18

    Enjoy the free drinks 18

    Get out & about 19

    Pack spares 19

Pack a mix of clothes 20

Chapter 2: Getting in & general overview 23

Getting In 23

General Overview of Las Vegas 26

Chapter 3: How to get around 29

Underground tunnels + bridges + shuttles 30

Buses 30

Monorail 30

Taxis 31

Chapter 4: Top 10 iconic Las Vegas experiences 32

Stroll down The Strip at night 32

The Aquarium @ The Mirage 33

The Erupting Volcano @ The Mirage 34

The Fountain show @ Bellagio 35

Shop 'till you drop @ The Venetian 35

Weekend brunch and gondola ride @ The Venetian 36

Ride the roller coaster @ The New York New York . 37

Catch a concert @ Caesar's Palace 37

Catch a Cirque du Soleil Show 38

    Gamble! 39

Chapter 5: Las Vegas' best landmarks 41

    The Strip 41

    Bellagio 42

    The Mirage 43

    High Roller 44

    Stratosphere Tower Las Vegas 44

    Fremont Street Experience 45

    Caesars Palace 46

    MGM Grand Las Vegas 47

    Red Rock Canyon 47

    Mob Museum 48

Chapter 6: Tips for a perfect girly weekend in Las Vegas 50

    Five is tops 50

    Pick the right mates 51

    Ideal time? 4 days 51

    Choose your pad wisely 52

    Play up your womanhood…in a good way! 53

    Plan for time out! 53

    Pack wisely 54

Update your research 54

Hit the pool clubs: they're cool, casual and very classy 55

Pack the sunscreen and skip the fake tan 55

Splurge..55

Guard your ID with your life 56

Hold back..56

Chapter 7: Best day spas in Las Vegas 57

The Spa @ Mandarin Oriental 57

Spa @ ARIA 58

Canyon Ranch Spa Club 58

Qua Baths and Spa...58

The Spa at Trump 59

Grandiose @ the Bellagio 59

The Spa @ Encore...59

Sahra Spa & Hammam..60

Chapter 8: Feast like a local 61

Chapter 9: Shop 'till you drop............................68

Forum Shops @ Caesar's Palace 69

The Grand Canal Shoppes @ The Venetian 69

Via Bellagio 70

Wynn Esplanade 70

Fashion Show Mall @ The Strip 71

Town Square Las Vegas 71

Miracle Mile @ Planet Hollywood 71

Crystals @ City Centre 72

Downtown Summerlin 72

Tivoli Village 73

Las Vegas North Premium Outlets 74

Las Vegas South Premium Outlets 74

Fashion Outlets of Las Vegas 75

Refinery Celebrity Resale Boutique 75

Souvenirs & gift shops 76

Chapter 10: Best Nightclubs in Las Vegas 79

Chapter 11: Useful References 83

Chapter 12: Cool Facts About Vegas You Probably Don't Know 85

**** PREVIEW OTHER BOOKS BY THIS AUTHOR**** 89

"FLORENCE FOR WOMEN: THE ULTIMATE TRAVEL GUIDE FOR WOMEN" by Erica Stewart 89

Chapter 1: What to know before you go

Las Vegas is one of those destinations that everyone *thinks* they know but, as it turns out, they don't. To help you navigate your way through Vegas, and help you best prepare for your trip, we've compiled an invaluable list of all the things we think you ought to know…before you go.

Yes. There is a seedy side to Vegas

This may not come as a big surprise to anyone, but it's still worthwhile pointing out that Sin City can actually be…a tad sinful. Adult attractions and services abound and you will encounter people who drank too much, gambled too much and got up to all sorts of shenanigans. Especially along The Strip. Oh…and people can still smoke everywhere here, due to Vegas having been granted special permissions in this regard. If you're sensitive to any of this, then a trip to Vegas is probably not for you. However, if you can just shrug it off and continue on your merry way, you'll have an unforgettable time!

Every hotel lobby is amazing

No matter where you choose to stay, you must make a point of visiting the A.M.A.Z.I.N.G. lobby of every hotel within walking distance. From gargantuan glass sculptures to tropical gardens complete with REAL tigers, the competition for 'most mind-blowing hotel lobby in Vegas' is very much a thing. Hotel lobby-hopping is a bona fide activity here.

Small and compact...but huge

Vegas may seem overwhelming at first – and it is – but do keep in mind that most people find a 'corner' they love and end up spending most of their time there. The trick, however, is to discover this corner *before* you even arrive. The last thing you want it to be hailing cabs at 4 am or walking forever every day just for lunch. Ascertain what you are likely to want to do and see, and then pick a hotel that's basically RIGHT.THERE.

Book early

The earlier you book...the cheaper the deals. Simple as that.

Best time to visit

Anytime around Christmas is crazy busy, crazy expensive but also crazy fun. July and August are the cheapest months to visit, but the heat can be unbearable – fine if you plan to spend most of your time in air-conditioned malls and resorts. Those few weeks between Thanksgiving and Christmas? Yep. Great and affordable too.

Research where you want to stay

This little tidbit of advice is arguably the most invaluable of all. You won't believe how many people book one hotel, only to find themselves spending most of their time just next door because it has the nicest pool, more eateries etc. Do your research and pick your favorite place, close to all the attractions which you want to see. Book it well in advance and you will score an unbelievable deal. Deals, in Vegas, are everywhere.

...but search for deals first

Many people erroneous think that the huge, opulent hotels in Vegas must cost a fortune. Fact is, hotel accommodation is not where these places make their money. You can find some truly amazing deals on hotel accommodation, with many offering rooms for as little as $50 a night, in the hope that guests will spend many times this amount on gambling, food and drinks. At the end of the day, if you set yourself a limit on your 'spending money' – but granted, you have to stick to it, even at 3 am – a Vegas vacation need not be an expensive treat necessarily.

Factor in the hidden 'Resort Fees'

Resort Fees are the sneakiest way for hotels to sneak in an extra daily expense, and ranges from $15 to $30 depending on the hotel. These are supposed to cover all the inclusions you'd normally expect, like wifi, access to the gym and pool, or daily newspaper at breakfast. In a way, this is a way of splitting the room rate in half, and making the whole deal seem much more appealing. Make sure to look for the fine print, under Terms and Conditions, as these charges are not usually clearly advertised. There are still some hotels which don't charge Resort Fees, but usually that's because they don't have a gym, pool, or breakfast bar!

On a tight budget? Stay Downtown...

Choose a Downtown hotel if you want to save some holiday cash, but make sure you choose a hotel which includes a free shuttle service to The Strip.

Use your usual 'common sense' safety precautions

Las Vegas is no more (and no less) safe than any major capital, so keep your wits about you and use commons sense. Don't go wandering off at night along dark alleys, keep your alcohol intake in check (especially if you're a solo female traveler), leave valuables at home and dress in accordance with how much)or how little) male attention you wish to receive.

Wear comfy shoes & use free shuttles

Yes, The Strip is only a couple of miles long, but the walking distances, for an entire day of hotel-hopping, can be humongous. Wear comfortable walking shoes and take advantage of all the free transport options you'll no doubt come across. From monorails, to shuttle buses and people-movers, there are many convenient ways to get around which don't involve catching a cab.

Enjoy the 24/7 life

Vegas-ites are always surprised when they travel elsewhere and discover they can't go out for dinner at 11 pm and find nowhere to buy munchies at 4 am. To them, these are all perfectly normal requests. All of the major hotels in Vegas will have a café, restaurant and bar which stay open 24/7, as do most of the convenience stores. So dare we say you'll never be left wanting for anything.

Look out for flyers and giant minions

While in all other cities people who hand out flyers are called 'people who hand out flyers', in Vegas they're known as canvassers and they have won special permissions to stand on footpath (and sometimes, in your way) to hand out flyers for whatever show/service/event they're paid to promote. Some visitors find them annoying but we find that a polite no and a walk-by is usually sufficient deterrent. As for the giant minions? Well, they're everywhere. Not only giant minions, but giant Marios, giant Elmos, giant

Cookie Monsters and what not. Costumed folks are all over the place but they only get annoying if you snap a photo of them and refuse to hand over a dollar. Other than that, they can be quite cute.

The traffic is manic

We're not sure exactly what it is; maybe it's too many neon lights, or erupting fountains, the giddiness of the pace or sheer excitement to be here, but both drivers and pedestrians along The Strip are deadly lethal. Watch out for the crazy traffic and use overhead walkways if you want to cross. Believe it or not, your biggest danger in Vegas is getting run over. This, and dehydration.

Drink plenty of water

Cocktails by the pool at 10 am, scorching temps during the day and big nights out. All of these things can contribute to a severe case of dehydration. Yes, we know that a peach bellini is more delicious than a glass of water, but for the sake of your health...keep hydrated!

Want to gamble? Take a class

Most of the gambling hotels offer free gambling classes to novice, first-time visitors. These classes are not only informative but are also super fun to take with a group of girlfriends. Moreover, if you do want to gamble a little but feel intimidated by the 'big timers', knowing how it all works will help you feel more comfortable.

Enjoy the free drinks

Well, considering you're being hit with hidden resort and 'entertainment' fees at every turn, it's really nice of the casinos to offer you free cocktails as you sit on the slot machines or play at a table. Go down for a quick gamble before dinner – and after – and you can enjoy a few delectable cocktails every night, at no extra charge!

Get out & about

There are some quite amazing attractions in and around Vegas, which aren't within the walls of an opulent hotel. Fight the urge to stay 'in' all weekend and explore the stunning Red Rock Canyon while you're here.

Pack spares

Las Vegas is one of the most aesthetically pleasing destinations you'll likely ever visit and you'll be surprised how snap-happy everyone gets here, yourself included. Bring spare camera batteries and memory cards and don't forget to put it all on charge, every night.

Research comp deals

Comp cards are offered by all of the major hotel chains, and they get you discounts, entry and free coupons for everything: meals, clubs, shows etc. Ask about a comp card at your selected hotel and see what's offered.

Las Vegas Pass

If you think you'll see a lot of attractions here – which require entry fee – then check out the Las Vegas Pass. It offers over $500 worth of discounts, but you need to ascertain whether it will worth the initial expense first. For most visitors, it is.

Show discounts

Check out this website for cheap last minute tickets to all the shows – especially in low season when seats need to be filled.

Pack a mix of clothes

Las Vegas can get quite chilly, especially when winds pick up, so although you'll certainly encounter some scorching daytime temps (you'll be in a desert, after all), you will need a jacket for cool evenings outdoors and to counter the effect of the over-zealous air conditioning in all the indoor complexes.

Need some help packing? Here are some invaluable items no woman should leave home without:

- Casual clothing – This is Vegas' best uniform, worn at any time of day or night. Yes, some people dress up, but being that this place is a hive of visitors from all over the world, you'll be perfectly dressed no matter where you go, as long as you're neat and tidy.

- One classy outfit – Because that 'dress up' person should be you...at least once!

- Sneakers/flip-flops/sandals & one pair of heels – And your feet will be well taken care of.

- Accessorize – make sure your necklaces and earring match with your bags and shoes, and you can turn one outfit four ways.

- Two bikinis and two cover-ups – for those gorgeous days in one of the pool clubs

- Hat and sunnies – make them ever-so-trendy if you must, but don't forget them. The sun is brutal out here!

- Hair dryer – first check to see if your hotel supplies it, then bring a small compact one if it doesn't.

- Travel size cosmetics – soaps, shampoo & conditioner: stock up on small travel size bottles and save a load of space.

- Ibuprofen & aspirin – fail safe drugs for that middle-of-the-night headache, when the last you fell like doing is getting dressed and taking 45 minutes to get out of your hotel.

- Converter – hailing from abroad? Buy at converter at the airport before you arrive!

Chapter 2: Getting in & general overview

Getting In

BY AIR

Las Vegas is serviced by the McCarran International Airport, one of the busiest in the whole country, and arguably the only one with slot machines in the arrivals hall. There are daily direct flights from many US cities, as well as connections to overseas destinations.

You'll find the airport just about in the centre of town, only a couple of miles south of the MGM Grand and Caesar's Palace. The airport has two terminals (1 and 3) which are quite spread out, so use the white and blue shuttle to hop back and forth.

A taxi to your hotel (if it's on The Strip) should cost about $10, and a ride to Downtown just shy of $20. You'll find taxi ranks outside exits 1-4 on T1 and on

Level Zero on T3, along with dedicated staff who'll help you grab a cab. A 10-20% tip is usually expected by drivers. There are also a number of different shuttles you can take, which are fast and convenient. The Group Shuttle is great if staying at a major hotel, and RideShare option is a quick and safe option which you can book through the Lyft app on your mobile phone.

Want to start your Vegas trip in luxurious style? Then we suggest you book a limousine service!

BY BUS

There are several coach companies which will take you to Vegas from just about anywhere. The most popular are Greyhound (L.A., Phoenix and Salt Lake City), LuxBus (L.A. and San Diego) and Megabus, which are gargantuan double-deckers with wifi and all the mod cons.

BY CAR

Vegas is only about a 4-hour drive from Los Angeles, making it a very popular weekend destination. In fact, the highway leading into Vegas (**Interstate 15**), on a Friday afternoon, is banked up for mile after endless mile. Not only is the traffic quite harrowing to deal with, but you should note – especially if you're visiting from abroad – that this stretch of remote desert highway was the deadliest stretch of road for over a decade, anywhere in the US. The problems are numerous. Together with speeding and reckless driving (which you can pretty much expect over a weekend, in both directions), the desolation means that if anything does happen, help won't be on the way very quickly. Driving to Las Vegas is not recommended if traveling alone, most especially when cheap flights abound. Besides, you won't be driving around once you reach the city *and* you'll likely be quite exhausted by the time you leave.

Now, having said all this…driving this stretch of road is actually lovely and you'll get to cross the Mojave

Desert and pass by a few very charming towns. Do this during the week and at leisure and it can make for a phenomenal road trip. Do make sure you always have plenty of water, food and petrol in the tank, and a few road trip buddies to keep you company.

General Overview of Las Vegas

Everything about Vegas can be a bit confusing for first-time visitors, who are planning their trip. Technically speaking, Vegas is only 'The Strip' (which actually makes it a very tiny town), yet nearby neighborhoods (which are technically cities in their own right) still use Las Vegas at the end of their mailing address to facilitate matters. Moreover, all of the following hoods as in the Las Vegas Valley. So…town, suburb or an entire county?

All of the above!

Yet no matter how far and wide the city really spreads, and at the end of the day, visitors to Vegas only stay in two areas: The Strip, or Downtown.

The Strip

When you think of Las Vegas, and envisage endless party nights, gambling addictions, flowing cocktails and head-spinning hotels...you're thinking of The Strip. This is the adult side of Vegas everyone comes to see, the part of the city that never sleeps, parties hard and sucks you in. If you're coming to Vegas to *experience* Vegas, then you have to stay on The Strip. No two ways about it. Here, you'll have all the major themed resorts at your fingertips, all the shows, casinos, restaurants and shopping. Squeezed between paradise and Spring Valley, The Strip is the epicenter of town, even though it's technically south of the Las Vegas city limits.

The Strip is just over 4 miles long and home to 15 of the world's 25 largest hotels. Check out this handy list of hotels on The Strip.

Downtown

Downtown is where Vegas started, all those years ago, and now offers a great glimpse into an old, bygone era, regardless of the continuous modern facelifts it receives. There are some great classic lounge bars in Downtown, the famous Fremont Street Experience entertainment quarter, as well as plenty of hotels, amazing shopping outlets and a huge array of restaurants to cater for all budgets. You'll find Downtown at the north-eastern end of The Strip, only about 5 miles from the epicenter of the casino resorts hub.

Chapter 3: How to get around

To help you get your bearings, when you first arrive, we recommend you hop on the Big Bus, the city's best hop-on/hop-off bus. It makes two dozen stops between Downtown and The Strip and can give you a fabulous overview of the main areas. A wonderful idea is to make one full loop with map and pen in hand, before getting off at your first point of interest. You can purchase 24 and 48-hour tickets and – if you pre-purchase your ticket online, get the two-day pass for the price of one. Check out the website for more deals and details.

Transport options, both in and from Downtown and along The Strip, abound; which is a great thing considering all maps of The Strip can be very misleading. Distance wise, this stretch of road is short and seems walkable, yet start exploring all the attractions and will find yourself exhausted, after a few hours, having barely covered 500 meters on a straight line. Luckily...there's plenty you can do to avoid walking-exhaustion.

Underground tunnels + bridges + shuttles

Due to the fact that outdoor walking can be hard work in the scorching heat, and the fact that hotels do their utmost to keep you in (and spending!), most of the hotels are connected to each other via a system of bridges, walkways and shuttles to facilitate getting around. Utilize them as much as possible and you'll enjoy your days much more.

Buses

Buses ply the route up and down The Strip, 24 hours a day. Tickets are $2 and can be purchased from vending machines at all designated bus stops. Refer to this online guide for schedule and itinerary changes.

Monorail

There's a monorail which runs on the eastern side of The Strip although of all that transport systems available, this is probably the least convenient. It runs along the rear entrances of hotels (so you still have to walk loads), breaks down often and costs $5 a ride or $15 for a day pass ($11 if bought online). To be honest, there are faster and cheaper ways to get around.

Taxis

The most convenient way to hop between hotels is to jump in a taxi, and this also becomes a cheap alternative to public transport if you're travelling here with your girlfriends. Do note that when traffic becomes congested on The Strip (which is often), taxi drivers will drive off to the side streets to save time, but this will add to your fare which is calculated in distance. Pick the best of two evils here: pay more, or take much longer, it's up to you.

Chapter 4: Top 10 iconic Las Vegas experiences

Las Vegas is a feast for all the sense, with innumerable attractions, shows and delights in which to indulge.

Here are the top 10 experiences which we really think you shouldn't miss.

Stroll down The Strip at night

The famous Las Vegas Strip is one of the most visited avenues in the world, attracting over 40 million visitors every year. This 4-mile stretch of road has a life of its own, a different vibe every hour of the day and night and gifts amazing and eye-opening experiences at every block. Taking a stroll is like going on a walk-around-the-world: not only will you see recognizable 'world attractions' but you'll rub shoulders with people from all walks of life and every corner of the globe. Cast your eyes on the Eiffel Tower, the romantic canals of Venice, the New York City skyline, fantastic fountains and erupting volcanoes. The Strip is THE place in Vegas at any time, yet taking your first stroll after sunset, and with the immensity of the neon-lights is simply spellbinding. THIS IS VEGAS, BABY!

The Aquarium @ The Mirage

Standing at the check-in counter of The Mirage Hotel is one of the most awe-inspiring things you could do in Vegas. Behind the desk, is a mind-blowing 20,000 gallon saltwater aquarium the likes of which you've never seen before – and will likely never see again. Keeping your mind on the check-in procedure will soon prove to be a challenge. Home to over 400 fish, the incredibly beautiful and colorful coral reef within the aquarium is like a slice of heaven in the midst of all the glamour and glitz of Vegas. The professional staff at The Mirage certainly understand that they are (literally) standing in front of one of the highlights of the city, so feel free to come and check it out even if you're not staying here.

The Erupting Volcano @ The Mirage

As if an entire miniature barrier reef was not enough, The Mirage also boasts a volcano. As one does. You certainly get a lot of bang for your buck (the attraction is free!) and luckily, this volcano erupts to schedule which is really rather convenient. Come along to watch Vegas erupt into a frenzy and you don't even have to worry about lava spills! Althoguh the volcano used to erupt every half hour all ay long, when it was first unveiled in the 1980s, the change in The Strip's topography, and addition of so many wonderful attractions, have convinced the owners of the Mirage to reduce shows to evening times only. The environmental concerns (it really does suck up quite a bit of energy) was a major motivator, and considering everyone visiting Vegas will stay at least one night (as if??!), this certainly has not taken anything away from this magnificent display.

The Fountain show @ Bellagio

Not to be outdone, the opulent Bellagio boasts the most impressive fountain show this side of…hmmm….the moon. Designed to 'romance your senses' the Bellagio fountain shows are one of the most popular attractions here, not irrespective of the fact they are free to admire. Perfectly choreographed to hypnotic lights and music, the shows are breathtaking in every way, and for everyone of any age, most especially when there isn't a speck of wind to be felt. Ambitious in design it may have been, but the concept and execution are simply perfect. Check out the website for show times.

Shop 'till you drop @ The Venetian

Imagine how amazing it would be if you took the awe-inspiring beauty of Venice and combined it with the shopping options of New York and the elegance of Paris? Well…head to the Grand Canal Shoppes at The Venetian and you can actually experience it. All of it. Half a million square feet of superlative shopping space. Nothing more, nothing less. Plus more food options than in all three cities combined, no doubt. The Grand Canal Shoppes is arguably the most addictive place in all of Las Vegas so do proceed with caution or you may never resurface. If only life were that fair.*Sigh*

Weekend brunch and gondola ride @ The Venetian

All the major hotels in Las Vegas try to outdo each other when it comes to putting on a comprehensive and delectable weekend brunch. While many do a 'good' job, a number are positively under par and a select few get it spot on. Of the last bunch, the Bouchon at The Venetian is the overall crowd favorite. Headed by a multi-award winning chef, whom Time Magazine voted 'The Best in the US' (he's originally French), the gastronomic emporium that is the Bouchon offers unparalleled quality, variety and ambience. Feast on mouthwatering Croque Madame, eye-watering chicken and bacon waffles and every dreamy sweet under the sun. brunch is served until 2 pm on weekends and, although ti may not be the cheapest you could have, it will certainly be the very best.

Ride the roller coaster @ The New York New York

The Big Apple Coaster is an-adrenalin-pumping ride at the New York New York Hotel with a mind-bending collection of twists and turns only found in one other ride worldwide. Pay your $14 ticket, jump on board and try to hold on to your heart as you begin with a 180-foot ascent, followed by a 76-foot drop, a mere reprieve, a further 144-foot fall, two inversions, a twisted dive loop, a 180-degree spiral and half-loop to round things off. Giddy much?

Catch a concert @ Caesar's Palace

Elton John, Rod Stewart, Celine Dion…these are just some of the famous names who have graced the stage at Las Vegas' most famous concert and entertainment complex. This 4-Diamond luxury hotel complex, squeezed in-between the Bellagio and The Mirage, has legendary status in Vegas, with its first tower built back in 1962. Nowadays, it boasts six multi-storey towers, with a total of almost 4,000 rooms, the largest of which stretch for a mind-blowing 1,00 square feet. The Colosseum, the venue of the main Caesar's Palace shows holds almost 5,000 spectators and was initially built in 2003 for Celine Dion's very first concerts. Since then, a myriad of world-famous artists have performed here, including Cher, Mexican sensation Luis Miguel, Dolly Parton, Julio Iglesias, Mariah Carey, Bette Midler, Harry Belafonte and countless others, It is often said that you only know you've made it BIG in showbiz, when Caesar's Palace lures you in for a string of concerts. Check out the headlining acts during your visit and score yourself a seat at this most historic concert venue.

Catch a Cirque du Soleil Show

If you're more of a Cirque du Soleil gal, then you're in luck. Las Vegas plays host to no less than eight incredible CDS shows, which have been entertaining crowds here for over two decades. Every show is themed and runs all year long, so if you're really busting to see a once-in-a-lifetime-performance, add this to your concert-gorging session. CDS is simply the largest, most famous and most magical theatrical production in the world! Ticket prices range from $59 to $99 and deals are offered whereby you purchase one ticket at full price and get the 2nd for only $15. Checkout the detailed show times here. Venues include the MGM Grand, Caesar's Palace, Bellagio and The Mirage. Every night, over 9,000 people watch a CDS show in Las Vegas…make sure you're one of them!

Gamble!

Alright…it's not like we were ever going to leave this out. Gambling and Las Vegas are synonymous with each other. The first casinos were built here in the 1930s and were simply meant to satisfy the entertainment needs of the thousands of workers who'd been brought in to build the Hoover Dam. No-one would have imagined, back then, that Vegas would turn out to be the largest and most famous gambling hub the world has ever seen. Without gambling, there simply would be no Vegas. If you're happy just betting a modest dollar or two then the world is your oyster in Vegas. You can gamble anything on any game, just about everywhere. There are even slot machines in some toilets if, you know, you can multitask like that. Slot machines are the most prolific gambling avenue in Vegas and yes, they are E.V.E.R.Y.W.H.E.R.E. Want to play with the big boys? Then heed our advice and take some free gambling lessons, provided by many of the hotels. Next, set yourself a budget, dress up to the nines and enjoy a super-fun night of gambling in Vegas!

Chapter 5: Las Vegas' best landmarks

To be honest, the reason we left gambling 'till last, on our previous chapter, was to simply highlight how diverse the attractions in Las Vegas really are. In fact, there is SO much to see and do here that if you do want to gamble, you need to plan in a time-out from all the sightseeing, people-watching, shopping feasting, hotel-lobby admiring etc etc etc....

While making your must-see list, here are the city's top attractions not to be missed.

The Strip

There's only one place where you should start your adventure in Vegas: The Strip. Renowned the world over for its crazy concentration of luxury hotels, resorts, casinos and high-rise apartment buildings, The Strip is a 4-mile stretch of Las Vegas Boulevard, considered the heart and soul of this vibrant city.

Although not too long at all, locals still refer to North, South and Central Strip, due to the sheer number of attractions on every block. A work in progress and an almost-living organism, The Strip's skyline is in constant change, with new attractions and renovations occurring at a head-spinning rate. The best thing to do here aside checking out EVEY hotel? People-watching, of course! The sheer cacophony of sites, sights and sounds make this one of the world's most entertaining 'roads' and will arguably be your number one point of interest.

Bellagio

Named after an idyllic Italian town set along the shores of Lake Como, the Bellagio resort is one of Vega's premier attractions and one of its most elegant hotels. Complete with replicated lake, home of the revered fountain show, the Bellagio is a feast for the senses. Take a step inside the lobby and look up: you'll see a ceiling covered in thousands of hand-blown glass flowers covering a total of more than 2,000 square feet. Aside the atrium and fountain show, you can see the Cirque de Soleil show 'O', the stunning conservatory and Botanical Gardens, and a Gallery of Fine Arts which displays priceless artwork on loan from various galleries from around the world. This resort has won the Five Diamond Award every single year from 2000 up until today, and chances are, it will continue to do so. Stunning, opulent and entertaining, this place will kidnap you for hours on end.

The Mirage

Visit Vegas and travel to Polynesia, just by taking a never-ending stroll through The Mirage, the world's most expensive resort ever built. Costing an eye-watering $630 million, the hotel is dusted in gold specs (no, really) and literally glows at any time of day and night. Renowned for its erupting volcano, The Mirage has quite a few notable attractions, including a rainforest in its atrium, a colossal aquarium behind its check-in desks, a Siegfried & Roy's Secret Garden and Dolphin Habitat, and Bare, a pool and lounge area which allows for topless sunbathing and is aimed specifically at women travelers.

High Roller

The world's tallest Ferris wheel is one of Vegas' latest additions and it is as astounding as the view it grants breathtaking. Over 500-feet in both height and diameter, the High Roller's an amazing ride which – if you can afford it – you should indulge in once during the day and once at night. The light show of Vegas-by-night is out of this world. This is the crown jewel of Caesar's Palace Hotel.

Stratosphere Tower Las Vegas

Want a phenomenal Vegas views with the ultimate adrenalin-rush? Then the Stratosphere Tower is the place for you. Part and amusing parcel of the Stratosphere Hotel, the Tower is home to a number of adrenalin-pumping rides and activities, including a heart-stopping 829 feet controlled-descent skydiving platform, a G-force pumping BIG SHOT, an insane

INSANITY ride which holds like a giant claw over 900 feet above ground and an X-Scream catapult. If the excitement and thrill of The Strip I simply too tame for you, then head up here for the ride of your life. Or, for the more sedate woman, the over 1,000 feet high observation tower may be just as exciting.

Fremont Street Experience

This is the best attraction in all of Downtown and certainly reason enough to stay here instead of The Strip, if you wish for a slightly more sedate, but equally brilliant, time. This pedestrian entertainment strip is actually a gorgeous look-back at the way Vegas used to be when it first started and this is the site of the very first hotel-casino ever built, back in 1906. The entire street is chock-full of bars, restaurants and shops, and there's an endless array of entertainers at any time of day and night to keep the crowds smiling. There are still plenty of casinos and more food than you could ever feast on, so head here for a brilliant time out and about.

Caesars Palace

Capping off the major-hotel trifecta, along with the Bellagio and The Mirage, Caesar's Palace is yet another gorgeous resort to check out. There's a fountain show, swimming pools and two nightclubs, as well as many famous concert performances, but what it's particularly revered for are the many top-notch restaurants manned by celebrity chefs. In total, there are 14 outstanding restaurants here, where you can savor everything for a $100 bowl of soup to a $5 slice of cake. The bacchanal Buffet has been rated as the best meal in town, and although it's not all that cheap it is rather spectacular. Amazingly, buffet here is served in individual little plates, rather than huge and messy trays, so the buffet looks as delectable as it tastes. There's the Gordon Ramsey Pub & Grill for amazing gourmet British comfort food with all the trimmings, and a NOBU outlet that'll make you swoon with glee.

MGM Grand Las Vegas

The largest of all the resorts (not just in Las Vegas but in all of the USA) the MGM is indeed a grand ol' dame. Up until recent renovations, the MGM was home to an African savannah enclosure, complete with half a dozen lions, and no boasts a Cirque du Soleil theatre, comedy club, a David Copperfield theatre, a Grand Arena for all major sporting and musical events, a day club and a host of bears and restaurants. The MGM casino famously boasts $1,000 a hit slot machines!

Red Rock Canyon

This amazing natural wonder is so close to Las Vegas that it can actually be seen from The Strip. Heading all this way and not adding a day's exploration here would be an absolute travesty. These amazing red-rock formations, set within the boundaries of a conservation area, are the region's premier rock-climbing destination and a spectacular natural wonder. Some of the walls rise up almost 1,000 feet and the contrasting colors make this an utterly photogenic place in which to spend an entire day. You can head here on a day trip organized through your hotel, but if traveling with girlfriends, consider renting a car and heading off on your own. It'

Mob Museum

The kind of culture for which Las Vegas is renowned is not exactly conducing to museum-openings, yet there is one side of the city's history that's definitely deserving of a little show-n-tell. The Mob Museum retraces the steps of Vegas through the decades: from its humble beginnings, to its life as a hub of organized crime and illegal ventures. Interestingly enough, the scope of this museum is much broader than first appears, and features not only the history of organized crime in Vegas, but also its branches all over the United States and the incessant efforts, by police forces, to bring them all to an end. Fascinating, disturbing and thrilling in equal measures, the Mob museum features mementos, stories, photos and paraphernalia dating back from the 1940s. Take a self-guided walking tour and get the inside knowledge of this most intrinsic part of Las Vegas' history.

Chapter 6: Tips for a perfect girly weekend in Las Vegas

Las Vegas is the perfect girl's weekend getaway destination, yet the sheer amount of things to see, do buy and eat means that planning a weekend here can get overwhelming, real quick.

Here are our best tips, hints and tidbits of advice, to help you plan a fun, safe and rewarding trip with your besties.

Five is tops

A five-strong group of girlfriends is fun, easy to manage and keep together and somewhat hassle-free. Plan to invite any more than four friends and you may end up regretting your decision. Five is the max which fits in a cab, easy enough to get a table reservation for and a comfortable number of buddies. Any more than that and you'll end up with two groups, which may be counterproductive to what you're probably envisaging.

Moreover, it's hard enough getting five people to agree on an activity, outing, restaurant and show...imagine having to do that with a small football team of peeps?!

Pick the right mates

It is common knowledge that every woman has different types of girlfriends. There are friends who's shoulder you cry on in times of trouble, friends you watch movies with, friends you have spa outings with...and girlfriends with whom you go to Vegas. Everyone has a different view on this city and they'd like to do once here. Make sure *all* of your views match to a tee.

Ideal time? 4 days

Stay in Vegas any longer and you'll be spending a whole day by the pool, followed by a very early night crashing in your room. Totally fine if you have the time, but it's still a lot of money to spend doing something you could do at home. Vegas is an assault for all the senses and you're bound to have a very intense time while there. Make it short and sweet.

Choose your pad wisely

It really pays to spend some time researching all the fantabulous hotels in Vegas, and choosing the one that's just perfect for all of you. And by all of you, we mean A.L.L. of you. Do not even contemplate splitting up your group and choosing two different hotels 'just because they're nest to each other'. Next to each other, in Vegas, means it could take you 30 minutes to walk from one room to another. Seriously! What should your criteria be? In our humble opinion, we think it best to choose just one favorite activity, and book your place accordingly. Whether it's the one with the most and best swimming pools, the one with the most shops, best restaurants, best value-for-money or most amount of slot machines, sleeping in the one place which offers the most/best of what you all want is by far your best choice here. Keep in mind that saving $10 on a room rate may mean spending $100 in taxi fares, so don't let budget determine your choice (too much) but don't blow all of it on accommodation either. Having little money to spend once you're here is sure to sour the mood for everyone.

Play up your womanhood...in a good way!

No, we don't mean you need to dress in mini-everything and always on vertiginous heels, but it means take advantage of your sex...in the nicest way possible. Groups of women are a highly-sought asset in clubs and many give discounts or free drinks to the ladies, in the hope that they will lure more big-spending men. Use it to your advantage and find out all the deals available before heading out for a party night.

Plan for time out!

Whether it's laying by the pool (no, without cocktail in hand), booking hour-long massages or enjoying each other's company over long and lazy lunches, making 'the sweet art of doing nothing' very much part of your weekend will go a long way in ensuring you don't crash and burn too hard and too fast.

Pack wisely

Remind yourself – and your girlfriends – to pack more than high heels and cute short little black dresses. You'll thank yourself profusely!

Update your research

Vegas is a gorgeous place to visit, but it's also a very transient one, where clubs, attractions, bars and restaurants go in and out of fashionable view at an alarming rate. The best reviews of places to visit and things to do and the ones which are made literally days before you travel. Smarten up and do your research, and keep it up while you're in Vegas too.

Hit the pool clubs: they're cool, casual and very classy

Vegas' pool scene is on par with its nightlife and set to actually take over and revolutionize the city's inherent character. Ok, maybe not, but the resort pools here really are out of this world stunning and are great places to socialize, enjoy bevies, dine, swim, sunbake and have loads of fun. Check out this online guide to Vegas' best pool clubs.

Pack the sunscreen and skip the fake tan

The first is an absolute must lest you fry yourselves silly, the second is just common sense!

Splurge

A fabulous haute cuisine meal, that mindboggling-buffet, or that amazing show and even the cool ride. Sure, you don't have to splurge on all those treats, but you should make a point of picking one, amazing splurge and making it the highlight of your girly weekend. The only catch? You'll need to get all the girls to agree on splurging on the same treat!

Guard your ID with your life

No matter how old you are, do NOT lose your ID or passport! If you do, you'll be very, very, very sorry. It's not only a matter of 'proving your age', having ID on you at all times is compulsory in clubs and casinos, so you just won't be allowed in if they do a random check and find you without.

Hold back

If it's enough to make your grandmother cringe...it's not suitable to post on social media. Just sayin'

Chapter 7: Best day spas in Las Vegas

Swear off the cocktails, shopping and awesome-sightseeing for a few hours and chillax in one of Vegas' most dreamy health and beauty spas. Mind you…this will not be your ordinary spa outing. Because as you may well guess, there are spas….and then there are Vegas spas, baby!

The Spa @ Mandarin Oriental

To prove that quality really does outshine quantity, the Mandarin Hotel Spa is about the most opulent beauty centre in Vegas, and one of its smallest, relatively speaking. There are still 17 treatment rooms, a hammam, relaxation lounges, a pool and foot spa centre, but what it lacks in size it more than makes up for in outstanding elegance.

Spa @ ARIA

Almost four times the size of the Mandarin's spa, the ARIA's beauty mecca is an 80,000 square feet space of gorgeousness complete with more than 60 treatments rooms, offering dozens of treatments, a fitness centre, stunning gardens with water features and an outdoor balcony that's to die for. Pay $30 and you get access to the facilities for a whole day.

Canyon Ranch Spa Club

Not to be outdone, the Canyon (which is twice as big as the Spa @ ARIA!) and includes a whole world of beauty and fitness. From a bona fide climbing wall, to a world class gym, fitness and yoga classes, a Jacuzzi, Finnish sauna, Arctic igloo (really!) and salt grotto...the Canyon offers you options you didn't even know you desperately wanted.

Qua Baths and Spa

The Caesar's Palace in-house spa tops it as one of the largest in Vegas, and boasts Roman baths, Vichy showers, more than 50 treatment rooms, fitness centre, herbal steam room and sauna, your own personal tea sommelier and even a snowy room with true blue falling powder.

The Spa at Trump

Unsurprisingly, the Spa at Trump stands just that step above the rest, with OTT treatments offered including massage oils infused with precious gem stones, facial creams made of crushed oyster shells and body wraps of treated seaweed. Do you really need this much extravagance. Of course you do!

Grandiose @ the Bellagio

Grand Grandiose is a phenomenal spa where both men and women are pampered in equal style. There are gorgeous whirlpools, steam rooms, and a fitness centre that's like a mansion in its own right.

The Spa @ Encore

This outlandish Orient-inspired spa is arguably one of the most awe-inspiring spaces in all of Vegas.

Glimmering lanterns adorn the ceiling and golden Buddha statues overlook the lobby, with the gold dust theme extended to the spa's amazing range of treatments. This spa is all about glamour, elegance and top notch treatments, so if you're after a superlative spa splurge then have it here.

Sahra Spa & Hammam

We have an affinity for themed spas, especially in Vegas where everything is just designed to perfection. This striking spa is like an oasis in the desert, both literally and figuratively speaking, and boasts an authentic Middle-Eastern hammam experience complete with rotating heated marble stone table…except there's very little in the Middle East which could actually compete with this beauty. Soak, steam, detoxify and get scrubbed and massaged into a heavenly bliss.

Chapter 8: Feast like a local

Oh look...it's feasting time again!

Spend but a day in Vegas and you'll soon realize what everyone who's been here has known all along. Vegas is not just a gambling and party mecca...this must surely be one of the world's most incredible foodies destinations as well. From cheap and cheerful to outrageously and famously expensive, there is something here to suit everyone. And by everyone we mean all seven billion people on our planet. Celebrity chefs run ahead with their über-famous joints, with plenty cool independent eateries grabbing their fair share of customers. Ever-famous buffets will never go out of style here and excellent bar food at pool clubs and lounges will ensure you never, ever, eeeeever go hungry when in Vegas.

Here's our top pick:

JAPANESE – Abriya Raku

When all the chefs from all of Vega's top restaurants come here to dine on their night off – even those of fellow Japanese restaurants – you know you're for the meal of a lifetime.

OF LAND & SEA – Andiron Steak and Sea

An intoxicating mix of excellent meats and outstanding seafood make this an insanely popular and very fashionable choice. Top notch steaks and oysters, grilled and shucked to absolute perfection.

FRENCH COMFORTY FOOD – Bardot Brasserie

Delectable French specialties which would make any French grandma very proud. A slicve of Paris in Vegas, complete with themes meals and cocktails.

ITALIAN – Carnevino

The name 'meat & wine' belies the true extent of the menu at this Italian establishment, which offers much more than just meat….and wine. Home-made pastas, super fresh sauces and delicious antipasti.

CHEAP & CHEERFUL GASTROPUB– Carson Kitchen

At less than $20 a main course, Carson can certainly be considered affordable here. Meals are generous and varied, with a load of focaccias, amazing sandwiches, shared plates and pub grub on the menu. Boutique brews and plenty of cocktails complete the picture.

ASIAN- District One Kitchen & Bar

Sure, you need to catch a cab to this eatery if staying on The Strip, but we can guarantee that the ride and fare will be more than worthwhile. Phenomenal Chinese, Thai and Vietnamese fare at very reasonable prices and in super cool surroundings.

JAPANESE-INSPIRED BURGERS – Fukuburger

Take the perfect American burger, add a dollop of wasabi infused mayo and special Fuku sauce and what you have is just the perfect combination of East and West.

SPANISH – Jaleo

Famous chef Jose Andres' Jaleo boasts an open-fire paella station and serves by far the best Spanish treats in town. Oldies but goodies, the tapas and paella here are out of this world.

ITALIAN WITH A VIEW – Lago

Bellagio's Lago serves up fusion Italian fare with more flair than you can imagine. Add a spectacular fountain view with your serving of *pasta fagioli e cozze* and you'll have a hard time deciding where to look. Choose from a wide selection of Italian tapas-style meals and take a culinary tour of Italy while sitting beside the most stunning 'lake' in Vegas.

HIGH ALTITUDE FARE – Top of the World

That Stratosphere Tower with all those amazing and hair-raising rides? Yep. It also boasts a restaurant. The views are the reason you should come, yet the food will surprise you even more. A delightful French-American fusion, the gastronomic delights here are – let's be honest – infinitely better than anyone would expect, considering the location would draw the crowds nonetheless. Breathtaking and delectable? Yes please!

BEST BUFFETS

Splurging on an all-you-can-eat feast is one of the most Vegas things to do. Along with gambling and show-watching, buffet dining (lunching & breakfasting too) is as iconic as it comes. There are near-endless options for buffet meals in Vegas yet, as with all things, not all are created equal. The best buffets in Vegas boast meat carving stations, wood-fired pizza ovens, salads and desserts galore and super fresh seafood. Yes. In the heart of the desert.

The best of the best?

Right here:

<u>Wicked Spoon @ The Cosmopolitan</u> – **Individually served portions, either in plates, spoons, terracotta pots or small frying pans, the delights here are perfect and just the right size. Try them all!**

<u>Bacchanal @ Caesar's Palace</u> – **Food that's fit for a Queen – or, in this case, an Empress, Bacchanal WOWs with its choice of nine different cuisines in a restaurants that's more showpiece than anything else. Italian, Japanese, Mexican, seafood…name it, and you can gorge on it here. Vegans and gluten-free welcomed!**

<u>Studio B @ M Resort</u> – **Simply sit back and watch while 200 incredible dishes are prepared daily before your eyes, on giant TV screens. Then…feast on them. This**

has arguably the best dessert buffet of the lot, in case you were wondering. Free flowing beer, wine and coffee make this a prime crowd favorite.

Chapter 9: Shop 'till you drop

Las Vegas may be renowned as Sin City yet all those who have ventured here soon realize that, in actual fact, it should be renamed 'Shopping City'. We challenge anyone to find a more comprehensive, exciting and varied shopping destination, anywhere in the world. The Strip, home to innumerable shopping malls, souvenir shops and dedicated boutiques, is a retail-world onto itself. If you endeavored to visit every single retail outlet along this avenue, you'd literally need years to see and buy it all. With an array of interests and prices, Vegas' best shopping haunts have something to offer every woman.

Here are the top shopping destinations in Vegas. Sure, you'll go home with an empty wallet...but at least you'll have plenty to show for it!

Forum Shops @ Caesar's Palace

With 160 retailers to choose from, the Forum Shops are a micro-cosmos that's almost impossible to leave. Shop, eat, shop, eat, shop....you get the point. The world's largest H&M store is here, as well as haute couture boutiques like Louis Vuitton, Jimmy Choo, Louboutin and many more. What makes this, the hands-down #1 shopping spot in Vegas, is the mix of affordable and splurge-worthy shopping, together with some truly excellent eateries like The Cheesecake Factory, Carmine's and Sushi Roku. Not to mention the spectacular tropical Atlantis Aquarium. Have only one chance for one shopping day? Make it happen here.

The Grand Canal Shoppes @ The Venetian

If you're looking for romantic flair along with an unsurpassed luxury shopping experience, then the Grand Canale's the place for you. Here, you'll find 875,000 square feet of spectacular commercial space, with dozens of up-market boutiques and designer stores, fine dining and, if that's not enough, picturesque cobblestone alleyways and canals complete with Venetian-style gondoliers. A gondola ride is an absolute must!

Via Bellagio

As one would expect, exquisite boutiques adorn the Bellagio Hotel's shopping arcade. When only the best will do – of GUCCI, Prada, Chanel, Armani and Fendi among others – Via Bellagio is for you.

Wynn Esplanade

Wynn is a bit of a winner, in our books, because although it's renowned for its high-end designer shops (you can actually buy a Maserati here, if you wish!) it also boasts one-off clothing and accessories boutiques that are actually within mere-mortals' budgets. Swoon and shop under one roof. It's probably one of the smallest complexes in Vegas– with only 20-odd stores – but also one of the most relaxing.

Fashion Show Mall @ The Strip

The Strip's largest shopping mecca, the Fashion Show is home to more than 250 boutiques and half a dozen department stores, including Macy's and Saks Fifth Avenue. We love the expansive food court and the many restaurants which cater for every budget.

Town Square Las Vegas

This is one of Las Vega's newest additions to the shopping scenes but is swiftly gaining a bit of a cult following here, especially among locals. Open air centre comprising two dozen separate buildings, plenty of entertainment and dining options, as well as hundreds of shops over an area that stretched more than 90 acres!

Miracle Mile @ Planet Hollywood

A 1.2 mile-long commercial extravaganza, the Miracle Mile offers shopping and entertainment under one roof. There are more than 150 shops, plus a dozen excellent restaurants and plenty of entertainment venues, stages and even a spectacular fountain show. There's certainly plenty here to keep you hooked all day long.

Crystals @ City Centre

Designer haven is about the best way to describe Crystal. If you want to shop, or just ogle, the most luxurious wares in the world, then this is where you'll need to head to. Italian, French and international famous brands boast boutiques here, and you'll also find plenty of gastronomic indulges too.

Downtown Summerlin

An all-in-one-emporium, the Downtown Summerlin is a mecca for shopping, dining and entertainment, spread out over a mind-boggling 1.6 million square feet of space. Over 100 boutiques and restaurants are found here, with retailers offering everything from clothing and accessories, to homewares and electronics. For a comprehensive shopping splurge, the Summerlin certainly fits the bill. This great outdoor district is a wonderful place in which to spend an entire day and night, with plenty of dining and entertainment options as well.

Tivoli Village

This is a gorgeous outdoor shopping experience, found about a 15-minute taxi ride from The Strip. If you have the time, and wish to experience something a little different, then make time to come here. A centuries-old European village – at least it *looks* like one – Tivoli is revered for its one-off boutiques of premium quality, and carries European brands most people have never even heard of. Beautiful clothing and accessories, plenty of al fresco dining and a charming shopping experience.

You're probably starting to think that the only kind of shopping Las Vegas offers is the ultra-expensive designer kind. You couldn't be more mistaken. When we said Vegas is one of the best shopping destinations in the world, we really meant it.

Here are some amazing outlet malls where you can shop till you drop…at a fraction of the original price.

Las Vegas North Premium Outlets

Of all Las Vegas' outlet centers, the North Premium Outlets mall is arguably the best, where you can find amazing stuff for up to 65% the recommended retail price, every day of the year. Choose from over 170 stores, including D&G, DKNY, A/X and Calvin Klein among many, many more. The only thing to remember, however, is that this is an outdoor mall and can get brutally hot in the middle of the day, so either beeline first thing in the morning, or set out a whole evening to shop in cooler temps.

Las Vegas South Premium Outlets

A slightly smaller and perhaps not-quite-as-good outlet mall as in the north, the South Premium Outlets offer great deals, nevertheless. There's a new outdoor promenade that's just delightful, but also many indoor sections so you can shop in lovely air-conditioned comfort.

Fashion Outlets of Las Vegas
Clothes, clothes and more clothes...that's what you'll find at fashion outlets, found about a 45-minute drive south of The Strip. There are more than 100 shops here – most of which are designer – offering discounts of up to 75%. If you're in a serious shopping odd then this is definitely worth the taxi fare.

Refinery Celebrity Resale Boutique
Second-hand designer gear, at fabulously discounted prices: that's the pull of this amazing shop. What's more, it also sells wares pre-loved by celebrities. It's a win-win, really.

When you've had your fill of fabulous fashions, take some time to check out all the great specialty stores in Vegas. Because there's plenty more where that came from!

Souvenirs & gift shops

Whether it's a Vegas key ring, snowball or tote bag, there's a souvenir that's right for you *somewhere* in Vegas. Here are the best gift-shops in town:

The Coca-Cola Store – The most iconic product that's arguably ever come out of the US, Coca-Cola has always had a knack for cashing in on its popularity. This two-storey emporium is no exception. More clothing, collectibles and accessories then you ever thought you wanted.

Houdini's Magic Shop – Watch your shopping funds magically disappear as you fill your basket with an overload of super cool stuff, like magic trick sets, illusions how-to books and DVDs.

M&Ms World – Devour your own body weight in M&Ms and fill your shopping bags with personalized flavored chocolate treats (they really do have your name on them!) for you and your friends.

Gamblers General Store – Probably the most apt souvenir to bring home, the gambling paraphernalia at this store is a perfect reminder of your Vegas trip. And not all of it is kitsch! Great quality gaming tables, customized chips, cards and all sorts of gear to recreate a mini-Vegas room at home.

Bonanza Gift Shop – A fabulous variety of your run-of-the-mill souvenirs, as well as some wonderful novelty items, Bonanza is the ideal shop to head to when you want to buy some souvenirs, but you just can't decide what! Come here and you'll definitely find it. This is rated the world's largest gift shop – at 40,000 square feet of space, it probably is.

ABC Store – There are 8 ABS souvenir shops in all of Las Vegas, offering everything from fine spirits to travel must-haves, local souvenirs, delicatessen treats, cosmetics, clothing and accessories. These shops are well priced and carry both necessities and souvenir-style items.

Chinatown Plaza – Vega's first Chinese-style mall is a great place to head to if you're in the mood for an infusion of exotic flavor to your trip. Great collectibles and fun souvenirs are to be found here– not to mention amazing food.

Chapter 10: Best Nightclubs in Las Vegas

Like to boogie? Well, you've come to the right place. Vegas is a party capital without exception and here you'll find some of the most outlandish, outrageous and over-the-top clubs you'll ever see, anywhere. Gold, bling, snazzy and even sleazy is the name of the game, with a club to suit every taste and budget.

Here are the very best nightclubs to check out when in Vegas:

XS @ Wynn Encore

The most expensive nightclub ever built, XS hosts some of the best known DJs from around the globe plus it boasts an outdoor pool area that's as dreamy as can be.

Hakkasan @ MGM Grand

Amazing 5 floor-dance emporium that's part nightclub and part gym (for the love of stairs!), this club boasts a gorgeous lounge area for when you need a sit and a chat with your buddies. Open on weekends only, and Thursday nights. This is the club all other clubs aspire to be when they grow up, so if you can only handle one night out, make it here.

10AK @ The Mirage

If it's good enough for a Kardashian NYE bash...it'll be good enough for you. Old world class and a fantastic Flashback Friday that's ideal if you're older than 25.

Marquee @ The Cosmopolitan

One of the few places which parties hard on a Monday night, drawing mostly visitors and plenty of locals who want to check out said visitors. Another gorgeous outdoor pool to accidently fall into. Oops.

Light @ Mandalay Bay

If you want to see, as much as be seen, then Light is the club for you. It joined forced with Cirque du Soleil and offers a phenomenal visual experience, complete with ceiling-dangling acrobats.

Tao @ The Venetian

A myriad of rooms for a myriad of different music styles and crowds. Plus a host of Asian delicacies at the restaurant. Double bonus. The most 'Vegas' Vegas club of all, Tao takes flamboyance to a whole new level.

Hyde Bellagio

If you need to 'hide' anywhere, go hide behind the fantabulous Bellagio fountains. Packed with VIPs and more class than arguably all the others combined, Hyde is where it's at for a small(ish) but very classy affair.

Sayers Club @ SLS Las Vegas

A hybrid between nightclub and live-music venue, Sayers is where all the cool gals hang out, for a more intimate yet no-less rocking night out.

Chapter 11: Useful References

Las Vegas.com: The official tourism site for Vegas, and one of the most comprehensive ever made. Long list of all the hotels and plenty of tips on what to do and see.

LasVegasUK: The official Vegas tourism website aimed at visitors from the UK.

LVWeekly: Greta resource for up-to date info on all that's happening in Vegas this week.

What's On: An invaluable free guide to all the happenings in Vegas. If your hotel doesn't supply it, ask your concierge to procure you a copy. You'll find coupons and discount offers aplenty.

ILoveVegas: Great resource with a host of tours/shows/tips and special offers.

Vegas4locals: Great resource offering deals, coupons and discounts on shows, meals etc.

CheapoVegas: On a tight budget? Look here for tips and advice on how to do Vegas for less.

EatingLV: Great, up to date restaurant reviews.

LVOL: The online entertainment guide to all the happenings in Las Vegas.

Groupon: Latest offers from Vegas...so start saving today!

Travelocity: Find great deals on Vegas trips.

Chapter 12: Cool Facts About Vegas You Probably Don't Know

Think you know all there is to know about Vegas? Think again!

Here are some interesting facts you probably don't know.

- While it's legal to generally drink in public places (although to do so within 1000 feet of a school or hospital will get you arrested) it is very illegal to drink from a vessel made of glass or metal. If the bar won't put it in a takeaway cup…don't walk outside with it!

- Prostitution is, lo and behold, illegal in Vegas. The local council also goes to a lot of effort to clamp down on illicit establishments in order to keep the city as family-friendly as can be. Wonders never cease.

- Gambling stops being legal just 25 miles away from the Strip!

- The man behind modern-day Vegas - the city of glitterati as opposed to one of gangsters and organized crime – was Howard Hughes. After collecting a vast fortune as a property mogul and movie producer, Hughes promptly arrived in Vegas in 1966, and proceed to buy an insane amount of hotels, right under the noses of the Mob. Many claim this to be the start of the end for Vegas' illicit era, and certainly the start of its golden years.

- There's a whole system of underground tunnels which runs the length and width of Las Vegas, and estimates predict more than one thousand people live there.

- In 1980, a local Vegas hospital uncovered a betting scheme within its wards, whereby nurses would bet as to when a patient would die.

- Spend but a single night in each and every hotel room in Vegas, and you'd need to stay there for approximately 290 years.

- All fountains and water features in Vegas use grey water, which is filtered excess water from sinks and showers.

- From outer space, The Strip is the brightest place on earth.

- About 30% of visitors to Las Vegas end up leaving without gambling a single cent.

- The largest sum ever won at a slot machine – with an investment of $100 – was $39 million.

- The Great Sphinx in Cairo, Egypt, is actually smaller than the replica built in Vegas.

- Visitors in Las Vegas, combined, consume more than 60,000 pounds of shrimp EVERY.SINGLE.DAY.

- The Bellagio Hotel, named after a small Lake Como town in Italy, has more rooms than the town has inhabitants.

**** PREVIEW OTHER BOOKS BY THIS AUTHOR****

"FLORENCE FOR WOMEN: THE ULTIMATE TRAVEL GUIDE FOR WOMEN"
by Erica Stewart

History and Culture

Any Florence travel guide can never be complete without detailing its rich history and culture. Our guide might specifically cater to our female readers, but it's still important to understand the area's history and culture, isn't it?

The history of Florence can be traced all the way back to the Etruscan times. The city was then known as Fiesole, one that dominated the entire region and was one of the most important Etruscan centers. As the Romans prepared for their war against Fiesole, they set up camp by the Arno River in the 1st century BC. This area was later called Florentia, which can roughly be translated to "destined to flower". Florence somehow managed to survive the Middle

Ages as well, and soon became one of the most important cities on the planet.

Florence's growth suffered a major setback because of a dispute between the Ghibellines, those loyal to Emperor Frederick II, and the Guelfs, those loyal to the pope. This led to the Guelfs being exiled from the city, but their absence was apparently short-lived, for they took over Florence once the Emperor succumbed to his death. Despite all the political turmoil, great attention was paid to arts and architecture, and this is one of the main reasons why Florence stands like a shining architectural jewel and a stark reminder of the romantic architectural wonders of a bygone era.

Art and culture were integral to the way of life as well. The desire of its locals to educate themselves led to the birth of the first works in the vernacular language in the form of "Dolce stil novo". This later inspired countless artists such as Boccaccio, Dante and Petrarca as well. In fact, Boccaccio's documentation of the Florence plague is one of the most accurate descriptions of a tragedy that began as dissatisfaction and ended with the "Tumulto dei Ciompi" in the year 1378.

Florence saw a small period where the people took over the rule of the city. However, this was evidently short-lived as the Medici dynasty soon took over. The Medici emperor Lorenzo il Magnifico was also responsible for much of the city's wonderful Brunelleschi architecture. After his death in the year 1492, the city once again fell into turmoil, but this era of conflict still managed to see the rise of world famous artists such as Leonardo da Vinci and Michelangelo.

From the 18th century up until the very beginning of the 20th century, Florence remained famous for its literary offerings and artistic wonders. It produced some of the best works of literature created by writers such as Palazzeschi, Papini and Pratolini, all of whom were members of the literary group "Giubbe Rosse".

Getting There and Around

Florence is well-connected to the rest of Europe and is easy to get into. It has witnessed a drastic increase in tourism over the past few years, and this has led to the development of all sorts of high-tech facilities and traveler-friendly infrastructure.

Getting There

The best way to travel to Florence is by air. The Aeroporto Firenze-Peretola is the main airport of Florence and is located at a distance of 2.5 miles from the city center. The ideal way to commute from the airport is to board the shuttle bus which connects the airport to the Santa Maria Novella station and runs at intervals of 30 minutes between 06.00AM and 11.40PM. Taxi services are available as well.

Getting Around

It makes sense to leave your cars behind while traveling to Florence. And even if you're coming from a faraway destination, forget all about that car rental. As women, one of our main concerns is our security, particularly when traveling to different countries. However, when it comes to Florence, you really don't need a car for most of its major attractions are located in its historic city center, an area best explored on foot (vehicles aren't allowed to enter the city center without prior authorization either). And visiting other destinations is easy as well, for Florence boasts of a decent public transportation system that lets you get from point A to point B without much fuss.

I recommend using the taxi services while in the city, particularly if you're traveling alone. Florence taxis are white in color and can be picked up from a taxi rank or be booked on the phone. Taxi ranks can easily be found in front of the main plazas and railway stations. Some of the top taxi operators in Florence include SO.CO.TA (+39 055 4242) and CO.TA.FI (+39 055 4390).

Florence is relatively small, and this means that a woman can really have a blast while exploring its streets on a bike. There are a number of cycle tracks in the city as well, and this certainly makes things easier. Some of the top bike rental companies to hire your bikes from include Alinari (+39 055 280500), Rentway (+333 9619820), and Florence by bike (+39 055 488992).

For women who like to keep it adventurous, the Segway offers a fascinating option of getting from one place to the other. It's convenient, it's simple and it's certainly super exciting. You can book your Segways by calling +39 055 2398855.

Finally, it is very hard to resist the romantic feel of riding in an open carriage. These enchanting rides transport you to a bygone era and Florence's enchanting cobblestone streets offer the perfect backdrop to relive yesterday. You can easily pick up a carriage in Piazza San Giovanni, Piazza Duomo and Piazza della Signoria.

Staying in Florence

Florence is one of the top cities in Italy for any woman wanting to choose from a wide range of safe, secure, exciting and inviting accommodations. Florence was among the first cities in Italy to develop its hotel scene, particularly because of the efforts of local designer Michele Bonan, who has now left his mark on hotels across the country, and the hospitality division of the Ferragamo Group, Lungarno Hotels.

Hotels for Every Budget

The city has always enjoyed a great tradition of hospitality and she takes a lot of pride in introducing her female travelers to some of its best-kept secrets. There's a lot of choice across all budgets, even in the historic city center, the place where you really want to be. Better yet, the competition amongst hotels keeps rates at a low, particularly during the off season.

For Ladies Wanting to Live like Locals

If you're dreaming of staying in an area that is full of artisan workshops, real people and hidden cafes, look no further than the Oltrarano district. Some of the top accommodation options include the cute B&B Floroom 1 and the Palazzo Magnani Feroni.

Billed as one of the top bed and breakfasts in the city, **B&B Floroom 1** is a sleek address located on the banks of the Arno River, and one of the top choices for solo female travelers looking for budgeted options in the city. This four-bedroom B&B boasts of an extremely relaxed atmosphere and each of its four rooms feature wooden floors, white walls, rustic ceilings and giant photographs of Florence. The old-new combination works quite well and really makes the property stand out. Some rooms also boast of four-poster beds, and an opaque glass wall hides away the comfy bathroom that has been fitted with pewter fittings and rainforest showerheads.

The **Palazzo Magnani Feroni** is one hotel that you'd never want to leave. It makes you feel like the nobility of yesterday and transports you to a historic location that makes you forget about everything else. Each aristocratic suite boasts of beautiful high curved ceilings and heirloom furniture and the terrace views rank among the very best.

For the Budget-Conscious Woman (Medium Range)

Casa Di Barbano is a simple option that offers great value for money. It is spacious and elegant and its owners are extremely friendly. All rooms are comfortable to say the least, and when you factor in the convenient location, safe accommodations, and reasonable costs, you have everything you need to explore Florence like a pro.

Casa Nuestra is one of the hippest addresses in the city. This brand new B&B is located close to the Campo di Marti station, and is characterized by its super friendly hosts. Apart from offering picture-perfect accommodations, the owners also go out of their way to assist you in planning your itineraries, show you how to explore the city and help you uncover enchanting walking paths.

For the Lady Who Travels in Style…. (Luxury)

Palazzo Vecchietti is one of the most elegant and beautiful hotels in the city. This boutique hotel boasts of stylish rooms, easy access to Via Tornabuoni and a superior level of service. The furnishings have been tastefully appointed, and great attention has been paid to every detail. Beds are comfy and usually include quality beddings and cashmere blankets. They are the just about the perfect places to snuggle into after a long and tiring day exploring the artistic wonders around the city.

Another popular option is the **St. Regis Hotel**. It boasts of a unique ambience that is both delightful and discreet at the same time. The hotel is located on an enchanting riverside location in centro storico and its Arno views appeals to female travelers who are accustomed to the highest standards of pampering. The service is warm and welcoming, professional and casual, discreet and attentive. Everything you'd want it to be. And the rooms are just what you'd expect from a hotel like St. Regis. I would recommend the Bottega Veneta suite, a top option for fashion-conscious women.

Things to See and Do
No matter how many times you come to visit this iconic beauty, you won't be able to see it all. A bridge on the Arno River is one of the first destinations that you should visit while in Florence. It is known to offer different experiences at different times of the day, for the views, the light, and the atmosphere changes each and every time. Considered to be the birthplace of the Renaissance, Florence also boasts of some of the best art and architecture in history. No wonder it manages to draw millions of tourists year after year.

Walking in the Footsteps of Michelangelo
Very few artists have managed to leave their mark on a city the way Michelangelo has in Florence. The city is home to some of his greatest masterpieces, and one of the biggest charms of visiting the city is to retrace his steps and explore places that are linked to his memories. Embarking on the following itinerary not only lets you retrace Michelangelo's steps, but also brings you closer to some of the most important arts and monuments in Florence. Remember, the ideal way to make the most of this itinerary is to spread it over two days, so that you get enough time to marvel at the various wonders and enjoy all that it has in store for you.

Start off your explorations at the **Casa Buonarroti**. Located in the vibrant Santa Croce, Casa Buonarroti is the palace where the artist's family lived. It was built by his nephew Leonardo, and passed hands from one member of the family to another until the iconic family finally became extinct. Casa Buonarroti hosts some of the earliest works of Michelangelo such as the *Madonna della Scala* and the *Battle of the Centaurs*. The former is a tribute to sculptor Donatello while the latter has been inspired by the Garden of San Marco. Both masterpieces were created by the artist while he was in his twenties, and imagining a young boy creating such outstanding works of art is an exciting experience in itself.

The next destination is the **Church of Santo Spirito**, another place that has been intricately linked with Michelangelo during his early days. Located in the Oltrarno district, the church is considered to be one of the most beautiful Renaissance-era churches on the planet. It was also the place where Michelangelo found accommodation after his patron Lorenzo de Medici died in the year 1492. The church is famous for its inspiring wooden *Crucifix* that Michelangelo created in the year 1493.

The next step of your journey takes you to the **Bargello Museum**. Michelangelo was forced to move to Rome in the year 1494 after the city riots sent Medici into exile, and it was in Rome that he created the world famous *Bacchus*, now located in the Bargello Museum. The museum is also home to other popular artworks created by the artist such as *David/ Apollo, Brutus,* and *Tondo Pitti.*

Don't forget to add the **Accademia Gallery** into your itinerary as well. Once Michelangelo returned to Florence in the year 1501, he set about creating some of his best works of art, including the outstanding *David*, now located in the Accademia Gallery. The Accademia is also home to many of his unfinished figures and sculptures. From the *"non finito"* sculpting techniques of *St. Mathew* to the marble wonder *Prigioni*, the Accademia truly showcases some of the most the distinct features of Michelangelo's style.

Head over to the **Uffizi Art Gallery** next. Considered to be one of the most famous art galleries in the world, Uffizi features a large collection of artworks created between the 12th and 17th centuries by leading artists such as Leonardo da Vinci, Botticelli, Raffaello and Giotto. The gallery also houses the *Tondo Doni*, Michelangelo's first canvas painting and the only of its kind in Florence.

Between the years 1515 and 1534, the Medici family saw two of its members becoming popes – Clement VIII and Leo X. Michelangelo was commissioned to create the *Laurentian Library* for the *Basilica of San Lorenzo* and the *Sagrestia Nuova* for the **Medici Chapels**. Both works of art are a must see and the entire complex is also worth a visit for its artistic ingenuity.

The last Michelangelo masterpiece that you should admire during your stay in Florence is the *Pieta Bandini*. This dramatic work of art was created in the year 1550 and is now located in the **Museo dell'Opera del Duomo**. It is considered to be one of the greatest examples of the master's work and what makes it even more special is his self-portrait, a male figure flanked by Mary and Magdalene, holding the lifeless body of Christ.

Best Neighborhoods

When planning any vacation, one of the biggest concerns for women is to choose the right neighborhood. There are some areas that have traditionally been famous for being safe for women, while ensuring that they don't miss out on the very best of nightlife and cosmopolitan delights that the city has to offer. When it comes to Florence, you need to decide between three choices – staying in the historic center, staying outside of the historic center or staying in the surrounding countryside. All three areas have safe neighborhoods for women, so it ultimately boils down to personal preference. Here are a few options to choose from.

Staying Within the Historic Center

The city center always dominates a major part of your holiday for most of the historic sights and attractions are located here. The area is among the oldest parts of the city, and the ring that you see is basically the spot where those 13th century walls were built. The city center is quite small, and car free as well. This means that you can easily walk from one place to the other and not miss a car throughout your journey. Staying close to the Santa Maria Novella station puts you within a 5-minute walk from the Duomo and staying close to the Duomo pits you within a 5-minute walk from Ponte Vecchio and Palazzo Vecchio. The ideal way to choose an area is to look for accommodations close to the sites you really like. Since most of the major sites are quite close to each other, I suggest staying between Piazza Santa Croce, Piazza San Marco, Piazza Santa Maria Novella and Pont Vecchio. This area is among the busiest areas in the city and is always full of tourists all through the day and in the evenings as well. The second option is to look for accommodations in the Oltrarno neighborhood, but that only works if you're leaning towards local experiences, unique furniture galleries and the Pitti Palace.

Staying Outside the Historic Center

With most of the restaurants, cafes, sights and attractions located within the historic center, you would argue if it makes sense to stay outside the center. However, many female travelers visiting Florence end up booking accommodations outside its historic center for all sorts of reasons. The biggest advantage of staying outside the city center is that it is friendlier on the wallet. Moreover, anyone wanting to stay in a residential area to explore the local way of life needs to step outside the touristic city center. A few areas that aren't really far from the main sights of the city include Via Bolognese, Fortezza da Basso, Poggio Imperiale and Piazza Beccaria.

Staying in the Surrounding Countryside

If you're thinking of keeping Florence as a base for exploring Tuscany, you might want to head over to the surrounding hills. Apart from letting you get up close and personal to nature, it also lets you enjoy all sorts of amenities such as gardens, outdoor areas and swimming pools in your accommodations without forcing you to pay through the roof. Having your own rental car is a must while staying in the outskirts, but it's perfect for exploring Tuscany to its fullest.

Manufactured by Amazon.ca
Bolton, ON